DEREK
The SHEEP
DANGER iS MY MiDDLE NaME

FOR JOHN ANDERSON

DEREK THE SHEEP: DANGER IS MY MIDDLE NAME

FIRST PUBLISHED IN GREAT BRITAIN IN 2020 by

BOG EYED BOOKS,
39 COPTEFIELD DRIVE,
BELVEDERE,
KENT, DA17 5RL

1 3 5 7 9 10 8 6 4 2

TEXT and ILLUSTRATIONS © 2020 GARY NORTHFIELD

COLOURING FOR PAGES 4-7 - RUTH TIMMINS-WILLIAMS
COLOURING FOR PAGES 36 & 37 - ELLEN LINDNER
"DANGER IS MY MIDDLE NAME", "SHEEPDOG TRIALS", "GRUMPA"
and "BEE BIG!" CO-WRITTEN WITH LAUREN O'FARRELL
WAYNE THE WHALE CREATED BY JACK ROWLANDS
"DIAL 'S' FOR STUPID", PUNCHLINE BY PETER STANBURY

THE MATERIAL IN THIS COLLECTION ORIGINALLY APPEARED IN THE BEANO AND BEANOMAX
BETWEEN 2007 AND 2011. THE RIGHT OF GARY NORTHFIELD TO BE IDENTIFIED AS AUTHOR and
ILLUSTRATOR OF THIS WORK HAS BEEN ASSERTED BY HIM IN ACCORDANCE WITH THE
COPYRIGHT, DESIGNS and PATENTS ACT 1988

PRINTED and BOUND BY COMICPRINTINGUK.COM

LOGO DESIGNED BY baxterandbailey.co.uk

BRITISH LIBRARY CATALOGUING IN PUBLICATION DATA:
A CATALOGUE RECORD FOR THIS BOOK IS AVAILABLE FROM THE BRITISH LIBRARY

ISBN 978-0-9955553-8-9

bog-eyed-books.com

DEREK
THE SHEEP

DANGER IS MY MIDDLE NAME

GARY NORTHFIELD

Bog Eyed Books

THE FARM'S MIGHTIEST HEROES

TO BEE, OR NOT TO BEE?

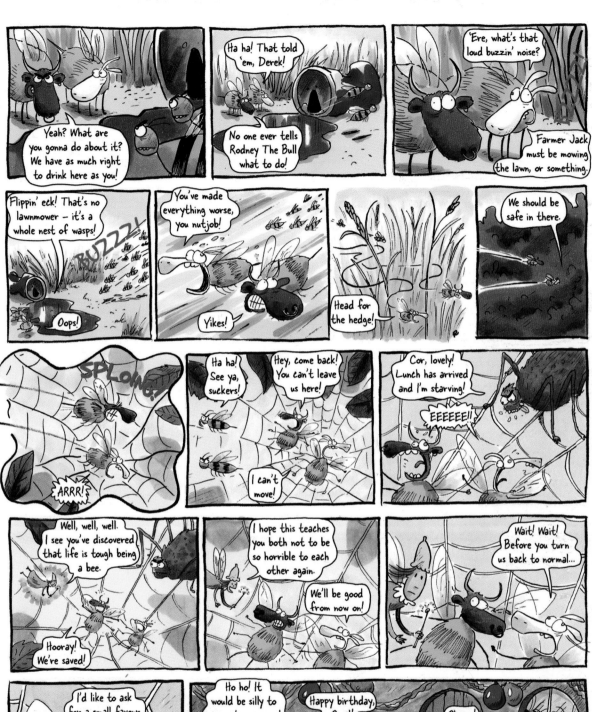

DIRE WOLF

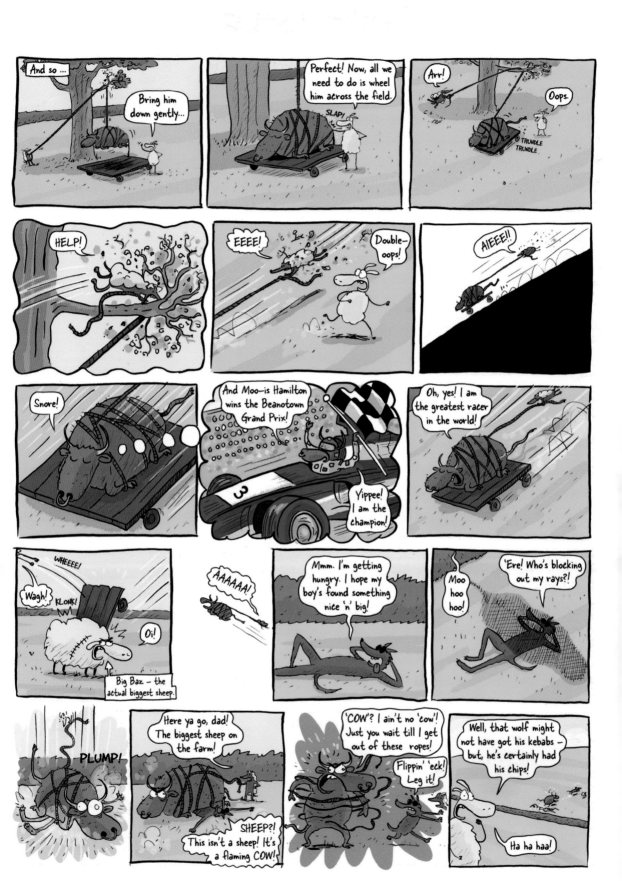

DEREK AND THE BEANSTALK

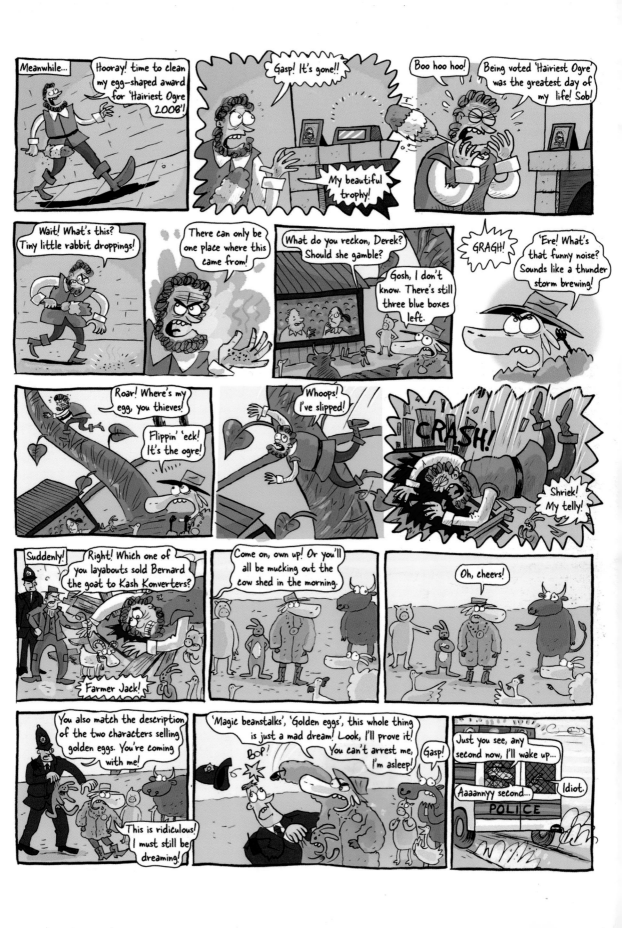

DANCING QUEEN

A WHALE OF A TIME!

Thanks to Jack Rowlands for Wayne The Whale!

DIAL 'S' FOR STUPID

TATTIES AND SHEEPS

DANGER IS MY MIDDLE NAME

SHUT YER CAKEHOLE

A HOLE LOT OF TROUBLE

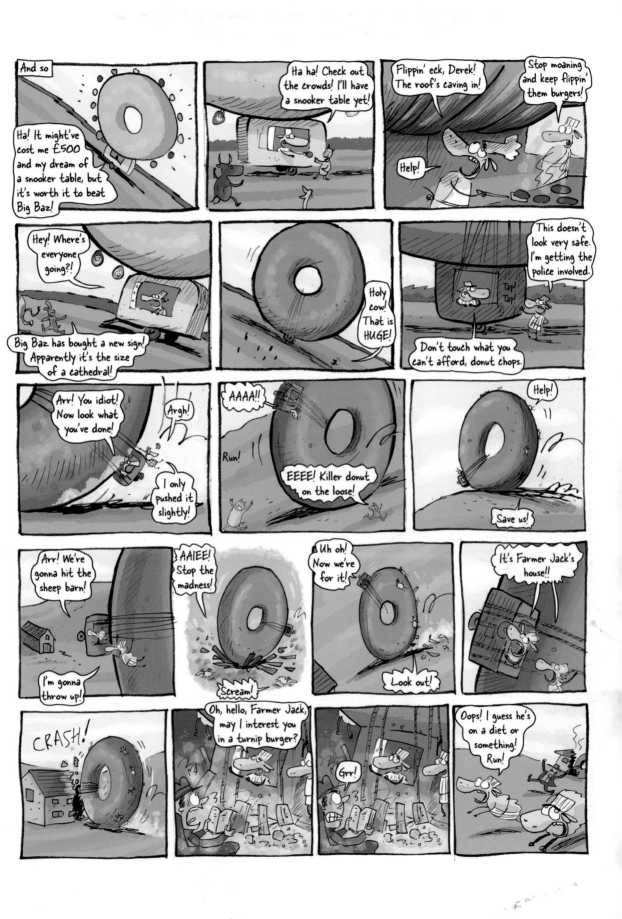

DATE FRIGHT

COME FLY WITH ME

SHEEPNADO!

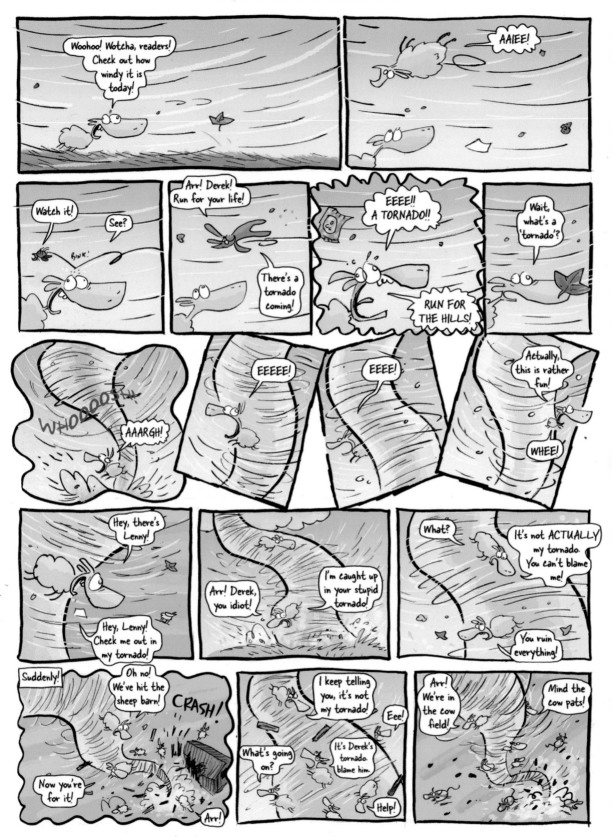

SHEEPDOG TRIALS AND ERRORS

One month later...

Come on, you lot! Put yer backs into it!

Whee!

Puff!

Peep!

Hup!

They're all yours, farmer Jack. Pushed to their physical peaks!

Good work, Clarence!

Your strict fitness regime should ensure my sheep win 'Flock Of The Year'!

That winner's trip to Bermuda is ours!

This is so unfair. We do all the hardwork and those two losers get the posh holiday.

I'll show them! I'm doing a runner! Who's with me?

?

But, I'm loving all this training, Derek. Check out my guns!

And I'm on the cover of He-Sheep!

Flex!

Flex!

HE-SHEEP

I can't believe no one wants to escape! Am I the only one who misses lazing about and eating cakes?

Forget about that, Derek, check out my amazing six pack!

Ok then, if we DO win this competition, I'm making sure we go on that holiday too! Who's with me?

Me!

Yeah!

Woo!

Will there be a gym?

And so...

Quick, Lenny, let's find the organisers and get this sorted!

FANCY PANTS

GRUMPA

SNOW JOKE

BEE BIG!

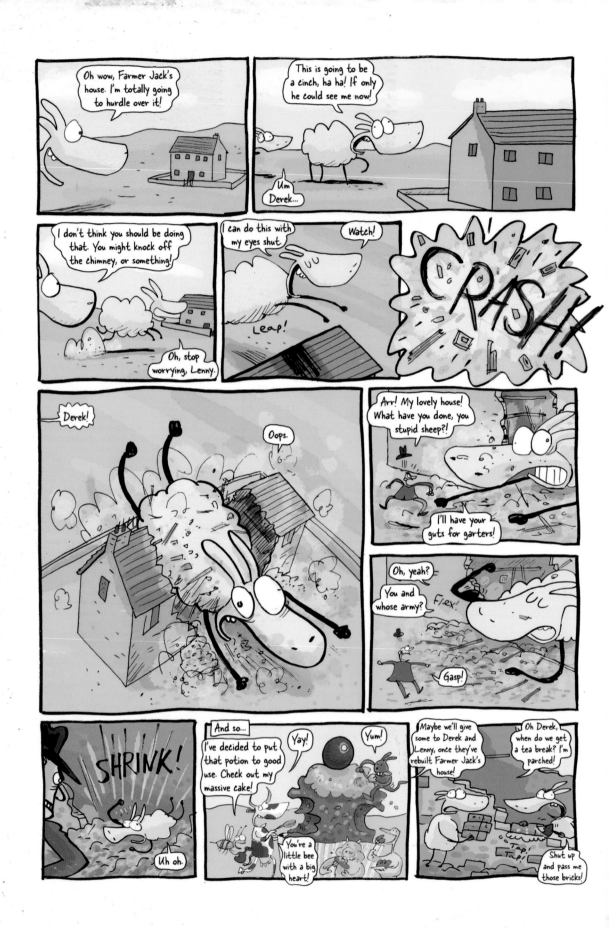